thelwell's
MAGNIFICAT

METHUEN · LONDON

First published in 1983
by Methuen London Ltd
11 New Fetter Lane, London EC4P 4EE
Reprinted 1983 (twice)
© 1983 Norman Thelwell
Printed in Great Britain
by Fletcher & Son Ltd, Norwich

British Library Cataloguing in Publication Data

Thelwell, Norman
    Thelwell's magnificat.
    1. English wit and humour, Pictorial
    2. Cats – Caricature and cartoons
    I. Title
741.5′942   NC1479

ISBN 0-413-53140-6

CONTENTS

THE MAGNIFICAT

Strong and silent, relaxed and independent,
the cat walks into people's lives and takes over.

All human beings seem either to adore cats . . .

. . . or to detest them.

They are quite content to live on . . .

. . . or off human beings – but only on their own terms.

They take whatever they can get – wherever they can get it –

– and feel no obligation to anyone.

Unlike dogs, cats stubbornly refuse to be taught how to do tricks.

Yet they are expert at retrieving game for their owners
– without any previous training.

By nature they are scroungers and layabouts, unwilling to move a muscle unless there is something in it for them.

If they think there might be . . .

. . . they can move like greased lightning.

They are inclined to be selfish when it comes to pleasing their owners –

– but can show affection quickly enough when they think the time is right.

Though the course of true love rarely seems to run smoothly for them –

– they are incredibly promiscuous.

And, although they like to hang about in unsavoury places
and stay out all night with questionable companions,

the cat is recognised above all other creatures
as the symbol of order and cleanliness . . .

. . . and the embodiment of homely warmth and relaxed contentment.

Cat owners' opinions may vary from time to time,
but there is one thing you can be certain of . . .

. . . they all know that they own the most intelligent
and beautiful animal in the whole wide world.

HOW TO GET A CAT

Kittens are the easiest of all pets to acquire.

There are usually plenty of people about
who are anxious to let kittens go to a good home –

– so think carefully before accepting.

Beware of pet shops that deal in sub-standard merchandise . . .

. . . or high-powered breeders trying to push their latest luxury model.

There are bound to be cats in your neighbourhood
already on the look-out for suitable accommodation . . .

. . . or anxious to interview prospective providers . . .

... but remember that once you commit yourself,
you will have a close companion for ten to fifteen years.

So, if you decide to adopt a stray, try to find its owner
before you get too fond of it.

35

Having made your choice, do *not* attempt to
carry him home in your arms . . .

. . . or inside your coat.

A good strong carrying-basket is essential for a relaxed journey.

CAT ABOUT THE HOUSE

Never take a cat home unless you are quite sure
he will be welcomed by the whole family.

He is bound to be a bit frightened at first –

– so try to confine him to one room for the first few days.

Kittens like to have their own sleeping quarters
with a blanket they can call their own . . .

. . . and a few little toys to play with.

Make sure his litter tray is kept in a convenient place . . .

... and that he knows exactly where to find it.

If you own a dog, don't introduce them too suddenly.

Given time to adjust, he will soon learn to play happily with other pets.

Tiny tots may not know the correct way to handle a kitten –

– so show them how it should be done.

Make him his own scratching-post or he might damage the furniture . . .

. . . and his own cat-door so that he can get in and out when he wishes.

Cats are very sensitive to loud noises – so never raise your voice . . .

. . . or lose your temper – remember he is a dumb animal.

Don't let him play in the garden for at least a week.

HEALTH & SAFETY

You will be surprised how little space your cat needs to keep fit.

You will find that however much he exerts himself he never sweats . . .

. . . or loses his poise and dignity.

You must learn to spot anything not quite normal in his appearance . . .

. . . or behaviour.

This will enable you to give an accurate description to your vet . . .

... so that he can treat the symptoms quickly.

Do not allow your cat to get into fights . . .

. . . or bitten ears may result.

Cats are as curious as children – so keep all medicines
well out of their reach.

Some house plants also can be poisonous to both.

Do not let him play with electric cables –

– and check all household appliances before you switch them on.

If you must bandage your cat, be patient with him –

– and try to gain his confidence before attempting
to remove a splinter from his paw.

It is advisable to seek assistance when administering pills.

INTERESTING BREEDS

THE MEXICAN HAIRLESS CAT
Thought by many people to be extinct. This may be due
to its embarrassment at being stark naked.

THE TURKISH SWIMMING CAT
Renowned for its love of water. It is an expert swimmer
and enjoys taking a bath.

THE TAILLESS MANX
Legend has it that it was the last animal to enter the Ark.

THE MALTESE
is believed to have given rise to the old joke
about the quickest way to make a Maltese cross.

THE BLUE SMOKE
is a very fast mover.

THE CHARTREUX
A French breed – very fussy about its food.

THE SIAMESE

is noisy, intelligent and quickly learns how to do tricks.

THE RAG DOLL
This unique Californian breed is so physically relaxed and limp
that it appears to need assistance whenever it wants to move.

THE BLUE PERSIAN

Its permanently morose expression is due to the fact that,
after washing all that hair, it can't do a thing with it.

THE ODD-EYED WHITE CAT
has one blue and one orange eye. It is said to be deaf
on the blue-eyed side.

THE SELF-COLOURED CAT
is a familiar sight in many homes.

THE RUDDY ABYSSINIAN
Though this is a distinct breed, the name
(or something very like it) is applied to many cats.

A CAT IN HELL'S CHANCE

Cats are reputed to have nine lives.
Unfortunately this is not nearly enough for most of them.

For example: many fall victim to their insatiable curiosity . . .

. . . or to their habit of leaping on any small furry object that moves.

They tend to take an unhealthy interest in ornithology . . .

. . . to hide in dangerous places . . .

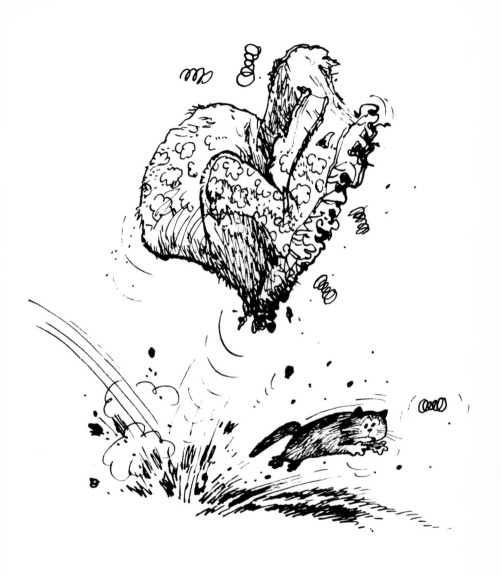

. . . and to rip up their loved one's furniture.

They take fearful chances in their devotion to drink . . .

. . . their addiction to tinned foods . . .

. . . and their love of late-night sing-songs.

They have a completely blind spot for road safety.

Cats are the only animals that insist on sitting on broomsticks . . .

. . . and sleeping on rhubarb.

They dice with death by climbing to high places . . .

. . . and doing dangerous balancing acts . . .

. . . but most of all by their high-risk methods of courtship.

SUPERSTITION

Throughout the ages the cat has had a unique place
in folklore and superstition.

The Ancient Egyptians worshipped it as a god –

– whilst in Medieval Europe it was feared and hated
as an incarnation of the devil.

It was said to be the favourite familiar of witches . . .

. . . and to have mystical power to foretell coming events.

Many people believed that cats were responsible for the weather . . .

... and could tell what human beings were thinking.

Throwing a sick person's bath water over the cat
was guaranteed to take the germs quickly out of the house –

– and if it sneezed near a bride on her wedding day,
then marital bliss would be her lot.

Some people even believed that a cat could tell exactly
where a human had been to purely by its acute sense of smell.

NEUROTIC CATS

Many cats suffer from strange neuroses of one kind or another.

They frequently see things which humans cannot see . . .

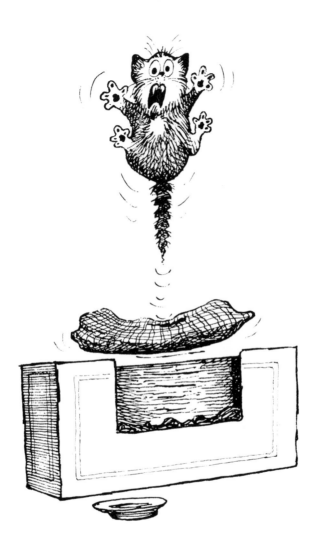

... and their sleep is sometimes disturbed by alarming nightmares.

They are quite likely to kidnap other small creatures
and lavish devoted maternal care upon them . . .

. . . or expect other animals to do the same for them.

They are well known to have alarming bouts of jealousy . . .

and premonitions of impending disasters.

There is no doubt that they are highly sensitive to atmosphere . . .

. . . and sudden vibrations.

Some owners even claim that their cats have psychic powers.

TIPS FOR TINY TOTS

Remember that it is a strange and terrifying experience
when a kitten is first taken away from its mother.

Try getting him used to a lead if possible –

– but, if you take him for walks on the lead,
try to avoid meeting dogs on the way.

He is bound to miss his mother's warmth at first, so make sure he has
a cosy, comfortable place to sleep . . .

. . . and some simple objects to hold his interest.

Bear in mind that your little pet must learn to attack and kill
early in life . . .

. . . otherwise it will not know what to do when it grows up.

Never put him out at night unless you are quite sure he wants to go –

– and make certain he knows how to get in quickly in an emergency.

Remember to brush and comb him vigorously every day
to avoid trouble with loose hairs –

– and never smack your pussy-cat when he has done something naughty.

Finally – the best known advice of all – if you move to a new home, do not forget to butter his paws to prevent him from running away.